Advance Praise for
Rewriting the Stories that Shape Our Lives

Rewriting the Stories that Shape Our Lives is a beautifully guided journey back to wholeness. With gentle wisdom and spiritual clarity, it offers a step-by-step path that feels both grounded and sacred. Each prompt is a mirror—revealing not just where you've been, but who you're becoming. It's not just a workbook; it's a companion for deep inner work, rich with reflection, honesty, and transformative truth. I didn't just complete exercises—I met myself.

—Mary Greene, Gahanna, OH

I'm not someone who usually reads workbooks like this, but I'm so glad I did. *Rewriting the Stories that Shape Our Lives* helped me see myself in ways I never had before. It made me realize that some of the things I've been doing for years—like putting others first, staying quiet, or blaming myself—actually came from old stories I picked up when I was younger.

What I liked most is that the workbook didn't talk down to me. It was simple, real, and gentle. It helped me understand why I act the way I do—and more importantly, it helped me feel like I'm not broken. I just needed to see the pattern.

For the first time, I feel like I can change how I treat myself, because I understand where it all came from. I didn't need a degree to get it—I just needed to be open. This workbook opened my eyes and made me feel more whole.

—Samantha Rizzo, Bensalem, PA

Rewriting the Stories that Shape Our Lives is developed through Tricia's experiences. As a companion to *The Stories We Tell Ourselves*, it offers a helpful guide to liberation from our own harmful and limiting stories.

—Katherine Jones, Fairborn, OH

While *The Stories We Tell Ourselves* reads like a suspense novel, *Rewriting the Stories that Shape Our Lives* gives everyone an actionable guide to get the most growth from their own challenges, enabling many to go from surviving to thriving.

—Rich Cordale, Columbus, OH

Rewriting the Stories that Shape Our Lives leads us on a beautiful spiritual journey as we "rewrite" the most sorrowful stories of our lives, transforming them into—yes, believe it or not—transcendent stories of love, gratitude, and forgiveness.

Tricia leads us by example throughout this step-by-step process by role-modeling for us her own rigorous and brutally honest process using introspection as her vehicle to uncover places of deep eternal gratitude hidden within the core of her being where she has found the strength to love and forgive not only herself for her own perceived failings, but also those who failed her. Lastly, for anyone (like me) who has endured extreme pain in their life, I wholeheartedly recommend both Tricia's memoir and her workbook, as I believe they provide for us not only an honest glimpse of hope, but also a transcendent path of light through even the darkest of our nights.

—Doug Fitzsimmons, Centerville, OH
Doctor of Physical Therapy

Rewriting the Stories that Shape Our Lives

A Guided Workbook to Identify, Challenge, and Transform Limiting Beliefs Into Lasting Change

Rewriting the Stories that Shape Our Lives

A Guided Workbook to Identify,
Challenge, and Transform Limiting
Beliefs Into Lasting Change

TRICIA BAXLEY

ethos
collective

Rewriting the Stories that Shape Our Lives © 2025 by Tricia Baxley.
All rights reserved.

Printed in the United States of America

Published by Igniting Souls
PO Box 43, Powell, OH 43065
IgnitingSouls.com

This book contains material protected under international and federal copyright laws and treaties. Any unauthorized reprint or use of this material is prohibited. No part of this book may be reproduced or transmitted in any form or by any means, electronic or mechanical, including photocopying, recording, or by any information storage and retrieval system, without express written permission from the author.

LCCN: 2025905328
Paperback ISBN: 978-1-63680-492-7
e-book ISBN: 978-1-63680-493-4

Available in paperback and ebook.

Any Internet addresses (websites, blogs, etc.) and telephone numbers printed in this book are offered as a resource. They are not intended in any way to be or imply an endorsement by Igniting Souls, nor does Igniting Souls vouch for the content of these sites and numbers for the life of this book.

Some names and identifying details may have been changed
to protect the privacy of individuals.

To you—
Whether you are just beginning,
returning once more,
or somewhere in the quiet, tender middle of your healing—

This workbook is for you.

For the part of you that's grown tired of old narratives,
that senses there is more to your story than pain or survival,
and that still—despite it all—believes in the possibility of peace.

May these pages meet you with gentleness.
May they offer language where there was once silence,
and space where old patterns used to live.

May they remind you that transformation is not about fixing what is broken, but about honoring what has always been whole within you.

You are allowed to rewrite your story.
To soften the voice of shame,
to speak to yourself in new ways,
and to create a life that reflects your truth—not your wounding.

And as you walk this path, may you know—
you are not alone.

With love and reverence,
Tricia

Table of Contents

Introduction xi
Exercise 1: Brainstorming the Past 1
Exercise 2: Organizing Memories 12
Exercise 3: Beliefs 19
Exercise 4: Writing Your Story, Part 1 33
Exercise 5: Limiting Beliefs 39
Exercise 6: Patterns 58
Exercise 7: Defense Mechanisms 66
Exercise 8: Labeling Defense Mechanisms 68
Exercise 9: Reflect on Relationships 71
Exercise 10: Write Your Story, Part 2 75
Exercise 11: Affirmations 81
Exercise 12: Anthem 87
Conclusion: A Return to Wholeness 93
Endnotes 95
Acknowledgments 97
About the Author 101

Introduction

It's not how you started your life, it's how you decided to live it.

This workbook gives a step-by-step process to healing your own childhood trauma and the limiting beliefs that others have programmed you to believe are true about the world and yourself. Research has shown that 95 percent of our beliefs are subconscious, and it's this subconscious programming that runs the show behind the scenes, out of our awareness.[1]

I believe that we are always whole on a Soul level; that the damage we believe about ourselves or others has convinced us that we are broken is untrue. Instead, there are "wet blankets," layers of beliefs that block our light and wholeness, which need to be shed to transcend to a place of Inner Peace, our birthright.

Your inner light and wholeness have always been a part of you; they just need to be uncovered. Wholeness awaits you, along with that inner peace, joy, unconditional love, and freedom from the false beliefs you have learned. *A Course In Miracles* refers to this as heaven on earth; why wait for heaven if heaven is now?[2]

Whether spoken out loud or just thought, affirmations have the power to change our subconscious. Before we embark on the journey of healing, we will begin the process of resetting our beliefs about ourselves. The idea is to reprogram from the very beginning, even if it feels uncomfortable at first.

Daily Affirmations

No matter my size, shape, or age, I am beautiful.
I am worthy of feeling deep, unconditional self-love.
I deserve to be treated with respect.
My boundaries keep me safe and are valid.
My intuition is a connection to my Higher Power, and I will find strength in listening.
All the answers I need are inside of me; I choose to listen to my inner wisdom and voice.
I will ask for what I need from my Higher Power, Spirit Guides, and Guardian Angels.
I know I am never alone.
I see the beauty in nature and feel my connection to all.
My inner light shines brightly even when I don't see or feel it.
It is my birthright to feel whole and loved.
I choose to live in Love and not fear.
I forgive myself for anything I have done out of fear vs. Love.
I forgive others for everything they have done out of fear vs. Love.
I feel gratitude for all that I have.
I will offer kindness to all who cross my path.
I do not judge myself.
I do not judge others.
I am enough simply by being.
I do not believe the false messages I have been told.
The people who hurt me did the best they could with the tools they had.
The only thing my Source asks of me is to be my most authentic Self.
I am emotionally strong and willing to be vulnerable.
I accept everyone as they are.
I will live this day with childhood wonder and curiosity.
I will choose Inner Peace over external wealth and materialism.
I will live today with a sense of deep hope.
I will pray for others.
I will pray for myself, knowing self-care begets self-love.
As a child of the Divine, I am good.

While affirmations alone can't change the faulty programming, they will help with the process. I would like each of you to say these affirmations at least twice a day. If it's workable, write them down and position them to be in your line of sight as soon as you awaken and right before you close your eyes for the night.

Focused Meditation

Often, when we are very stressed and distracted, saying something as simple as an affirmation can be challenging. One tool to help you get into a positive vibration is focused meditation. Included in your workbook is a custom mandala that I created with sacred geometry and the vibrations of Unconditional Love, Inner Peace, Divine Light, and Joy.

Mandalas have been used for centuries to help create better alignment with our energetic bodies, activating our potential and expanding our minds. A mandala is a symbol of the Universe in its ideal form, and its creation signifies the transformation of the Universe from suffering into one of joy. We will use the mandala as part of your focused meditation. You can recite the affirmations before, during, or after.

1. Place the mandala in a spot that is easy to see and where you can intently focus without distractions.
2. Find a comfortable place to sit, such as a chair or on the ground.
3. Loosen your shoulders and arms and take slow, deep breaths from below your ribcage. Be as fully relaxed as you can without falling asleep.
4. Once you are fully relaxed, turn your attention to the mandala, focusing on the colors, geometric patterns, and its overall shape. Allow yourself to be fully present in the present, paying attention to the sensations you feel, continuing to breathe slowly and deeply.
5. Allow any thoughts that enter your awareness to come in and then leave. Try not to make any judgment on the thoughts; allow them to come and go. Focus on the sacred geometry of the mandala to help you connect with your spirit and the Divine Light within. The mandala colors have been chosen to represent:

    - rebirth, renewal, vibrant health (green)
    - inner peace, intuition, the Divine (blue)
    - gratitude, grace, and joy (rose)

    Allow the colors to wash over you as you direct your focus.
6. If you find your mind having difficulty quieting down, still make no judgment, acknowledge it, and return to the present moment. At first, the present moment might be 5–10 minutes, hopefully building up to 30 minutes to start your day. Meditation is a fabulous way to reach our higher self, which is the source of Love and Joy and wonderful inner guidance.

To download your free mandala, visit APath4Healing.com/mandala or scan the QR code below.

I realize not every childhood is dysfunctional. If you are embarking on the journey to tackle this workbook, I will assume you have limiting beliefs and blocks that are holding you back, feel stuck, and that you want to heal.

Physical and sexual abuse, parental/family addiction, absent parents, loss of a parent(s) through death or abandonment, chronic illness of self or parent or family member, poverty, and mental health issues are all very visible signs of possible dysfunctional childhood environments.

Others are less overt: enabling, expecting too much, being praised for the outcome vs. the effort, being placed on a pedestal, and for those who are unsure, since too often dysfunction passes as normalcy, I will first list the qualities of a healthy family environment and then list the qualities of toxic parenting and families that often slip under the radar.

Healthy Family Characteristics

- They provide physical and psychological care for their children. They do not expect the children to take care of parental emotional, psychological, or physical needs.
- They provide an atmosphere of safety and security where there is no fear of emotional, psychological, physical, or sexual abuse. Parents can allow their children to express their full range of emotions in ways appropriate for their age.
- They have consistent rules that are explained, and boundaries are honored.

- They allow all members of the family to be and express their authentic selves in a supportive manner.
- They create an environment of respect for all family members and are flexible to meet the individual needs of each family member.
- They set age-appropriate responsibilities that are both forgiving and flexible to each family member.
- Perfection is never the goal; instead, focus on the effort behind the goal.
- Family members can fail and fall without enabling behavior in a supportive environment.
- Parents praise children for their effort and hard work, rather than the finished result.
- Adults apologize for mistakes, so family members learn the art of admitting when they are wrong or when they have hurt someone.
- Talk, listen, and connect. Allocate time to be present with no interruptions to engage in active listening. Know your child's life, including outside relationships.
- Parents see their child as they are, not as they want them to be.
- They discipline effectively, consistently, and kindly.
- They encourage each family member to express gratitude and appreciate the value of what they have received.
- They show kindness to others. Service is a learned behavior; teach service early on so it becomes a way of life for all family members.
- They understand that every child is unique and never make comparisons with others.

Toxic Parenting Characteristics

- They do not allow the expression of negative emotions.
- They are critical. Nothing you do ever meets the standards set before you.

- They make every little positive thing you do seem like a monumental accomplishment; this creates a need for external validation and a false sense of self-worth.
- They don't allow you to fall or fail, always smoothing over emotional pain so you never develop resilience.
- Praising the goal over the effort sets a child up to believe that nothing less than perfect is good enough, even if they give their all.
- They do not understand that every child is unique and makes comparisons with others. This sets up the stage for a lifetime of wondering if you are good enough.
- Seeking emotional support from a child creates a blurring of the parent-child boundary where the child feels responsible for the parent's emotional states. This can lead to codependency issues in later relationships. This also prevents the child from learning and developing healthily.
- They use sarcasm or "jokes" at the child's expense. This affects a child's sense of self-worth and value and can lead to accepting abuse in later relationships since it feels familiar.
- Their lack of positive mirroring and a sense of safety leads to an adult who does not know who they are. They are not clear on what they value or what their life goals are, and often seek relationships based on a fear of abandonment rather than Love. Love becomes a need vs. a want. This can manifest as being avoidant or detached, or anxiously attached. Both prevent a secure form of bonding and an authentic expression of Love. This can lead to manipulative behavior and accepting toxic behavior and having weak boundaries.
- The underlying belief is that there are never enough resources to go around, so I have to grab as much as I can.
- Normalizing toxic behavior allows the child to have cognitive dissonance from a very early age—they know it's wrong, but everyone around them is acting as if it's okay. This dissonance in childhood sets up a lack of inner trust in adulthood, which leads to someone who can not trust their own inner guidance. They can be easily manipulated, will allow terrible treatment,

settle for less, and create toxic relationships that mirror their childhood.
- They don't support your goals. When a parent undermines what you want to achieve, they create a belief that goals are impossible to achieve. This often sets the adult up for underachieving and not being willing to reach their full potential in both career and relationships.
- They have a "love me but fear me" attitude, demanding unconditional Love from a child but causing psychological or emotional fear at the same time. This invalidates a child's emotional responses and prevents them from developing an inner compass of who is safe and who isn't. This leads to an adult who struggles to trust others, creating a dynamic of "walking on eggshells" that often carries over into adult relationships.
- Their lack of empathy, respect, and boundaries carries over into all adult relationships as a learned behavior and limiting beliefs about themselves.
- They destroy a child's property or take their belongings without permission; this creates blurred boundaries in adulthood or a hoarding mentality from feelings of lack.
- They invade personal privacy; blurred boundaries create distrust, and this carries over into adult relationships and expectations.
- Family isolation does not teach proper social skills or conflict management, and it creates a dynamic of enmeshment versus interdependence in adult relationships.
- Weaponizing children causes extreme guilt and shame in a child that undermines their sense of self. This affects their ability to form healthy relationships with others and a sense of lack within themselves.
- Conditional love creates emotional holes. Children believe they are only good for what they do, which can lead to extreme codependency and seeking fulfillment outside themselves..
- Secrecy causes extreme shame that the child buries deep within themselves, and it affects every aspect of the child's and adult's

life until they release it. The shame that isn't the child's own yet becomes a part of how they see themselves, and often it's buried so deeply that they are unaware. This causes an adult to achieve as much as they can to prove their worth. Or often give up early, all stemming from a deep sense of unworthiness. Relationships fill the emotional holes instead of adding more joy. Adults with these limiting beliefs often find themselves in one toxic or abusive relationship after another, recreating the same wound they experienced in childhood.

Even the most conscious parent will probably not achieve these positive parenting goals 100 percent of the time. To coin the term "good enough parenting," the goal is to come close, and this applies to social environments as well.

For many of us, our parents did not show these positive parenting qualities, and if we learned them, we learned them because of what I call the "what-not-to-do" form of parent modeling. When we learn early on that our parents are deficient, we stop trusting in their ability to teach us, and we teach ourselves.

A positive example of this is when someone becomes a responsible child because their parents are so irresponsible. The downside is that this often leads to over-responsibility, taking on the fixing of others, believing we do not need others, and creating wells that protect us, all to the detriment of ourselves.

Two important lessons are not to blame or feel victimized despite the programming. The important thing is to recognize where your parents, caregivers, teachers, or social environment fall short and not fall victim to the false beliefs they taught you.

Rewriting your story is the goal, reprogramming your belief system to what is true, away from the falsehoods you were led to believe were true. Once we realize we are operating from a false belief system that originated in childhood, when we were not emotionally or psychologically equipped to look at things from a mature perspective, we can then choose to look at life from the perspective of our Higher Self. No longer are we operating from the wounded self we needed to protect

Social Environments That Influence Self-Esteem

- **Bullying:** Bullying can leave lasting emotional wounds. Were you the victim of bullying? Did you have someone "safe" to tell and support you? How did you handle this? Were you the one bullying? How did this impact you?
- **Friend groups:** Fitting in, finding a group where you can be authentic. Did you feel like a part of the community of your school, or were you a loner/outcast? Did you participate in social activities like prom, sports, or other school-wide activities?
- **School environment:** Beliefs about one's intelligence. Were you supported intellectually or made to feel you were lacking?
- **Physical challenges:** Physical or learning challenges can shape how we see ourselves. Did you have a chronic illness/disability that set you apart, such as acne, learning challenges, ADHD, ADD, dyslexia, etc.?
- **Beauty standards:** Relying on beauty to be a barometer for one's worth. Was beauty a focus while growing up, being programmed to believe in an unattainable beauty standard, and comparing oneself to others physically?
- **Sports/Clubs:** Being part of a team or club can shape our sense of belonging and identity. Did you take part in sports/clubs, relationships with teammates, coaches, and advisors?
- **Teenage romance:** Teenage romance often teaches us about love, boundaries, and self-worth. Did you have a partner? Were you able to keep boundaries? Was there respect? Could you be authentic? Did your friendships support your beliefs and values? Did it end kindly or with a lot of drama?
- **School:** School can be a powerful influence on our sense of safety, identity, and confidence. Did the school promote self-discovery? Was it driven by fear-based discipline and rigidity? Did you feel supported academically? Did you feel safe with educators, administrators, and staff? Was there a resource or person you could go to if you needed support?

- **Religion:** Religious and spiritual environments can deeply influence our beliefs and sense of self. Did you feel supported in your place of worship? How did the message(s) impact you? Were your personal beliefs upheld? Were you allowed to question? Did it reflect who you are?
- **Financial status:** Our family's financial situation can impact our sense of security, opportunity, and self-worth. Was your family able to meet basic needs? Were you thought of as rich or poor? Did you have to contribute financially to the household? Did your family have the resources to support your passions? Was there enough disposable income for your parents to feel at ease? Was there financial stress in the home?

Every person in a dysfunctional household is affected, despite outward appearances. Often, those who are successful by society's standards fall under the radar because of their financial success, accumulation of material things, and perceived emotional well-being. They can appear responsible, resilient, self-sufficient, and empathetic—all qualities society values and measures as successful.

Despite appearances and being successful by society's standards, I was fully convinced I was not impacted by my dysfunctional childhood until later in life. This was the furthest thing from the truth. The positive influences were accurate, though at times, they bordered on a way to control my environment and even others. These are traits I still have, but they are more balanced.

While I was successful outwardly, I was perishing inwardly, living a life of quiet desperation and not quite understanding why, since I had everything I could ever want. The problem is that this was coming from ego and not my Higher Self. The truth is, I had nothing.

I had lost connection with my inner guidance, my Higher Self, and my connection with the Divine, and ultimately, I was living on an island amongst billions of people. It wasn't until my ego and all the well-defined defenses were stripped away after my husband's death that I could see how far off course I had gotten. It was at that point that my spiritual journey sped up.

My hope is that for those who read my book and follow the steps in this workbook to spiritual healing, you can avoid the need for a traumatic event to wake you out of your sleep, illusions, or false beliefs and find your way back home without having to suffer years of trials and tribulations. I am very certain this is possible; this is the path I took and found the Inner Peace I had been seeking my entire life, but didn't realize it was missing and inside me all along.

On a Soul level, we all have the inner strength, intuition, inner knowledge, resiliency, self-love, forgiveness, non-judgment, and a connection to everyone and our Divine. I used to have gratitude for my incredible resilience, and while I am still grateful, I now know that the true blessing is discovering we all have what we need, and it did not single me out. My ego made me believe in my "specialness."

My Higher Self reminded me that we are all whole. I have seen the poorest of the poor living in absolute squalor but at peace, and I have seen the richest of the rich empty and searching for one more thing to buy for the momentary high to fill an otherwise empty existence.

We are not all born externally equal, but our Higher Selves are the source of all we need, and we all have the same access. In this respect, we are all internally born equal. Not that we don't need the basics of food, water, shelter, and safety, but past the basics, we have the inner ability to find the higher-level needs, such as what Abraham Maslow described as our needs for belongingness, self-esteem, and, for some, self-actualization.[3]

Too often, our family of origin and society have convinced us we need to keep accumulating to be happy, particularly in our Western culture. For some, the chosen path may be material wealth, which is not wrong. It's the attachment to those things that causes the problem.

When we attach to anything outside ourselves, making it a need rather than a want, we create an inner belief that we are only as good as the things we have: the car we drive, the person we love romantically, our careers, the success of our kids, etc.

The problem with this is that fulfillment comes from the outside in, rather than the inside out, and we create our identity around these attachments. This works fine until the Universe sends a curveball, such as being fired from a lifelong career or losing all one's wealth in an investment that didn't work out, or, in my case, my husband's death by suicide.

When something catastrophic happens and we identify with what we lost, we easily forget who we are. This is precisely what happened when my husband died. I was so enmeshed in the world I had created (I believe we create the world ourselves) that I no longer knew who I was. I literally had to start over, figuratively having to learn to walk and talk again.

Not that we shouldn't love deeply and work hard for the things we want; it's just essential to not lose who we are at our core. In my case, I felt lost long before I left my childhood. I just didn't realize it.

To truly move forward authentically, it has been my experience that we must go back and uncover the beliefs we were taught about ourselves, life, and love, as well as the expectations we have in relation to everyone else and the world. This could bring up some deep emotions, so it is important to recognize that what could hurt you as a child can no longer hurt you as an adult.

Regardless of your reactions to what you experienced, please keep in mind that as a child experiencing some very traumatic things, much of how we reacted was simply survival techniques to keep us emotionally upright. At any point in time, we were doing the very best we could with where we were and the tools we had available.

Prelude to Exercise 1

To begin this exercise, please allow yourself to be in a calm, uninterrupted space so you can focus on your feelings and recapture some of your memories that you might have pushed aside. If things become too intense, take a break, do some deep breathing, and see if you can move forward. If it's still too intense, give yourself permission to come back when you are ready.

In my grief-facilitating work, Dr. Wolfelt has coined a term called "dosing," which applies to this kind of work.[4] Dosing is simply a term to feel emotions in a way that is comfortable for you to prevent overload.

To undo the false programming you have experienced, you too will need to grieve the negative messages you were told, the beliefs you bought into, the abuse you might have suffered, the attack on your physical and emotional boundaries, and the lack of unconditional love and safety from those who were supposed to protect you.

We often take these unconscious beliefs into every decision we make, from career choices to platonic friendships and, most frequently, into our romantic attachments, subconsciously hoping and praying that we can find the love, affirmation, and support we never had. Sadly, what typically happens is that we find a partner who feels familiar, familiar being the same script we learned about love in childhood. This type of attraction can feel magnetic, as if there were some sort of destiny at play. Often, though, what is at play is the familiar wounding and the hope that maybe this time we will be seen, chosen, and loved. More often than not, it is your inner child reacting to the woundedness from childhood. It is one of the goals of this workbook to recognize these attachments for the valuable lessons they serve, and to heal the woundedness so that relationships can now be entered into from a place of wisdom, rather than from a place of woundedness.

We need to change our script and our programming. It was false in childhood; it is false now. The difference in childhood is that your little self needed to do whatever was necessary to survive, and now your adult self has the skills and maturity to let your inner child know that they are safe and that you will allow no one to treat them in that manner again.

Each time you do these exercises, if you feel a sense of anxiety or even fear, take a moment to speak to your inner child and let them know that you have their back, that you will never leave them, that they are seen, that they are safe, and that they are loved unconditionally. This might feel awkward at first. After all, many of us have never heard these words spoken to us by anyone, but persevere through the uncomfortable feelings, and you will find ease and comfort in dialoguing with your inner child.

Our inner child still exists within each of us. It's the source of all our joy, innocence, happiness, and playfulness. The goal is to recover that which was hidden from us in childhood—the programming that covered our Higher Self and Inner Light with "wet blankets."

I want to mention here that this is not an assault on parents and their parenting. Again, we all do the best we can at any point in time. My parents failed me terribly, but they did the very best they could where they were; I'm certain if they had more to give, they would have. Whether you hold your parents on a pedestal, see them realistically, or disown them because of the damage they have caused, part of your healing is forgiving yourself and forgiving them.

Remember, forgiveness doesn't mean you have forgotten; it means you have chosen to let go. It means you have simply chosen to release negative feelings of resentment, vengeance, anger, hurt, or whatever other negative energy lives inside of you. The goal of these exercises is to raise your energy to a place of higher vibration and lightness. Any negative energy serves to keep you stuck and tethered to the past.

It's time to cut the emotional ties that bind you to your past and find a future untethered to the limiting beliefs you believed to be true, giving you the freedom to discover the peace and unconditional love that are our inherent birthright.

Exercise 1

Brainstorming the Past

※

IN THIS EXERCISE, we will brainstorm the past. After clearing your mind of all inner thoughts, I would like you to go back as far as you can, starting with the first memories you have from childhood, whether good or bad, and write them down. I want no thought or judgment on what you write. Simply write it down—bullets are fine—and move on to your next memory.

Your mind is going to want to stop you and to ponder, so, if possible, try to avoid any thought about what you're writing. The goal here is to be as authentic as possible and to allow yourself the freedom to remember in a very non-attached way.

Remember as much as you can from your earliest memories, and then progress from there. Write every memory that comes to mind on the worksheet below. Do this exercise from young childhood, early elementary school, through elementary school, early middle school, middle school, early high school, late high school, early college or early working life, to later college or work life and adulthood.

Try not to edit anything, no matter how hard or what you might deem embarrassing. In the end, it's all the same—there is no judgment, it is simply part of your story. If you are fully in the moment, you might do this in one sitting; for others, it might take several sittings.

Again, do not edit your memories, do not judge them, and do not emotionally attach to them. Write them down and move on to the next one that comes up.

Earliest Childhood Memories

Early Elementary Childhood Memories

Late Elementary Childhood Memories

Early Middle School Memories

Late Middle School Memories

Early High School Memories

Later High School Memories

Early College or Career Memories

Later College or Career Memories

Adulthood

Exercise 2

Organizing Memories

✸

ONCE YOU HAVE completed the first exercise, it's time to organize your memories. Again, this should be done with very little to no emotional involvement or judgment. Use the categories to arrange your memories chronologically, including both positive and negative memories from family or caregivers, friends, teachers, coaches, youth leaders, and others in positions of authority, as well as religious teachings and your own actions.

The last category is "other" for unique circumstances. Again, some of you might do this exercise in one sitting; others might take longer. Remember, life's journey is not a race. Keep your own pace and take as much time as you need.

Family/Caregivers

Positive Memories:

_____
_____
_____
_____
_____
_____
_____
_____
_____
_____

Negative Memories:

_____
_____
_____
_____
_____
_____
_____
_____
_____
_____

Friends

Positive Memories:

Negative Memories:

Teachers, Coaches, Youth Leaders, People in Authority

Positive Memories:

_____
_____
_____
_____
_____
_____
_____
_____
_____
_____

Negative Memories:

_____
_____
_____
_____
_____
_____
_____
_____
_____
_____

Religious Teachings and Experiences

Positive Memories:

_____
_____
_____
_____
_____
_____
_____
_____

Negative Memories:

_____
_____
_____
_____
_____
_____
_____
_____
_____

Your Own Actions

Positive Memories:

Negative Memories:

Other

Positive:

Negative:

Exercise 3

Beliefs

✹

NOW, THE HARD work begins. Each of these memories has created a belief about who you are and how you think people see you. Some of these beliefs can be positive and very productive, while others can be negative and very inhibiting. Some may be positive from society's perspective, but, in fact, are a hindrance to your own Soul's Truth.

The next exercise is to identify what each of these memories has taught you about yourself, which dictates your current beliefs and how you interact with the rest of the world. Ideally, we are born into a family and environment that promotes bold options; the italicized choices show the negative message a dysfunctional family teaches us.

At all times, please do not judge your answers, yourself, or others. The goal here is to help you release unwanted, limiting beliefs and remove any residual childhood shame or feelings of unworthiness. Each reaction is a defense mechanism that helps you survive, and often is no longer serving your highest and best good as an adult. No judgment.

The following is a list of these beliefs. For each of your memories you wrote down in the previous exercise, select the appropriate positive or negative memory that applies. Remember not to judge or dwell on it; just label it and move on to the next belief.

ACCEPTANCE

- I am loved for who I truly am, not who I pretend to be.
- I don't have to change myself to be accepted.
- My uniqueness is celebrated in my family/community.
- It's okay to have different opinions—I am still valued.
- Being myself feels safe.
- Even when I make mistakes, I am still worthy of love.
- I belong, even if I stand out.
- *I have to hide who I really am to be loved.*
- *If I don't act the way others want, I'll be rejected.*
- *Love is conditional—I'm only accepted when I behave a certain way.*
- *I need to perform or succeed to be liked.*
- *Parts of me are unlovable or too much.*
- *No one really gets me, so I have to pretend.*
- *I'm only safe when I'm pleasing others.*

SELF-CONTROL

- I can pause and choose how to respond when I'm upset.
- I was taught to name my feelings instead of acting them out.
- I learned that my actions have consequences, and that's okay.
- It's safe to slow down and think things through.
- I am proud of my ability to stay calm under pressure.
- I do not feel shame when I make mistakes.
- *I have no control over my emotions or actions.*
- *I fear punishment when I make a mistake.*
- *If I don't react instantly, I'll be hurt or ignored.*
- *I can't trust myself to make good choices.*
- *Anger is dangerous — I either explode or shut down.*
- *No one ever showed me how to manage big feelings.*
- *I fear being overcontrolled or left to figure things out alone.*

EMOTIONAL REGULATION

- I feel my emotions without shame.
- I name and soothe my feelings.
- I believe that big emotions are natural and manageable.
- I feel safe expressing sadness, anger, or fear.
- I have calm responses during stress.
- I feel supported, not silenced, when I have emotional needs.
- *My emotions are too much for others to handle.*
- *Crying or showing emotion makes me weak.*
- *I bottle things up to avoid being a burden.*
- *I feel shame for how I feel.*
- *I have to hide my emotions to stay safe or loved.*
- *I do not know how to calm down when I feel overwhelmed.*

CURIOSITY

- I ask questions and explore the world.
- Wondering "why" is celebrated.
- My creativity and ideas are met with interest and support.
- Learning is exciting, not something to fear.
- Mistakes are part of discovery, not something to be ashamed of.
- Books, nature, and imagination are part of everyday life.
- *Asking questions makes me seem annoying or disrespectful.*
- *I need to stop daydreaming and "get real."*
- *Exploring new ideas feels unsafe or discouraged.*
- *Curiosity is met with ridicule or silence.*
- *Wondering "why" made me feel like a problem.*
- *I accept what I am told, not to explore beyond it.*

GRATITUDE

- I appreciate even the small things in life.
- Gratitude is something I model to others.
- I say "thank you" and mean it.

- **Gratitude is linked to joy, not guilt.**
- **I notice what is good, even in hard times.**
- **Being grateful helps me feel more connected to others.**
- *I believe I should be grateful even when I am hurt or uncomfortable.*
- *Gratitude is used to silence my needs or complaints.*
- *I feel guilty for wanting more, because I am "supposed to be grateful."*
- *I feel shame if I don't immediately show appreciation.*
- *Gratitude feels like a performance, not a feeling.*
- *Expressing dissatisfaction means I am ungrateful or selfish.*

OPTIMISM

- **I believe things will work out, even when they are hard.**
- **I look for the silver lining.**
- **I believe that better days are always possible.**
- **Hope is something I practice, not just preach.**
- **I know that setbacks are temporary, not the end.**
- **I am surrounded by people who look forward to the future.**
- *I never get my hopes up.*
- *If things are going well, I am waiting for the other shoe to drop.*
- *Optimism feels naïve—I believe it is safer to expect disappointment.*
- *Dreaming big only led to big letdowns.*
- *Being hopeful makes me feel foolish or unrealistic.*
- *Pessimism feels like protection in an unpredictable world.*

KINDNESS

- **Being kind to others is valued and encouraged in my home.**
- **I see kindness and treat others with compassion.**
- **Helping others makes me feel good about myself.**
- **Kindness is seen as strength, not weakness.**
- **Kindness creates connection and trust.**
- **People notice and appreciate when I am kind.**
- *Kindness makes me a target—people take advantage of me.*
- *Being kind means ignoring my own needs.*

- *Being kind is the only way to be loved or accepted.*
- *I see kindness as weakness—I need to toughen up.*
- *No one shows me kindness, so I don't believe it matters.*
- *I have to earn kindness by proving myself.*

SELF-LOVE

- **My feelings and needs matter.**
- **I feel loved for who I am, not just for what I do.**
- **I speak kindly to myself.**
- **Mistakes don't make me feel unworthy—they help me grow.**
- **I take care of myself emotionally and physically.**
- **I know I don't have to earn love—I already have it.**
- *Loving myself is selfish or arrogant.*
- *I have to be perfect to be lovable.*
- *My value comes from what I do for others, not who I am.*
- *I criticize myself constantly because I was criticized often.*
- *I believe self-love is vanity, not worthiness.*
- *I don't know how to take care of my emotional needs.*

FORGIVENESS

- **Everyone makes mistakes—including me.**
- **Forgiving doesn't mean forgetting, but releasing pain.**
- **I model forgiveness through honest conversations.**
- **I talk through hurt instead of holding grudges.**
- **I understand that forgiving myself is part of growing.**
- **Forgiveness is a part of Love and includes compassion and repair.**
- *I believe forgiveness means letting others hurt me again.*
- *No one ever apologizes, so I bottle my anger.*
- *I have to earn forgiveness by being perfect.*
- *I don't deserve forgiveness for my mistakes.*
- *Forgiveness is used to silence me, not heal me.*
- *I am told to "just get over it" without being seen or heard.*

AUTHENTICITY

- I am accepted for who I truly am.
- I don't have to pretend to be someone else to be loved.
- My feelings and thoughts are welcome, not judged.
- I express myself honestly.
- I feel safe showing my true self at home and with friends.
- I am confident I will find my tribe.
- *I hide parts of myself to be accepted.*
- *I believe being liked means being who others want me to be.*
- *I feel unsafe expressing how I really feel.*
- *My true self feels unsafe, so I create a false self.*
- *Fitting in was more important than being real.*
- *When I am honest, it causes problems—so I stop trying.*

CONFLICT MANAGEMENT

- It's okay to disagree and work things out calmly.
- I talk through problems respectfully.
- Conflict can lead to understanding, not just pain.
- It is safe to express anger or frustration without being punished.
- Apologies and repair are a necessary part of relationships.
- *Conflict always means someone is going to get hurt.*
- *I shut down or run away when things got hard.*
- *Being angry makes me a bad person.*
- *I have to scream or lash out to be heard.*
- *There are no healthy resolutions—just silence, avoidance, or explosion.*
- *I believe that expressing my truth would cost me love or safety.*

ABUNDANCE

- There is enough for everyone, including me.
- I trust that my needs will be met.
- I believe that generosity attracts more good.

- **Abundance is measured in love, connection, and creativity, not just money.**
- **I feel supported by both people and the Universe.**
- *There's never enough—I have to fight for what I get.*
- *Only certain people get to have good things. I'm not one of them.*
- *Wanting more makes me feel guilty or selfish.*
- *I believe I have to earn love, safety, and even basic care.*
- *Life is hard, money is scarce, and joy is a luxury.*

RESILIENCE

- **I can get through hard things and come out stronger.**
- **Mistakes and failures are how I grow.**
- **I try again even when things feel impossible.**
- **Asking for help is a form of strength, not weakness.**
- **I believe that no matter what, I can find a way.**
- *If something is hard, it means I'm not good enough.*
- *I have to push through everything alone—no one will help me.*
- *I believe I have to be tough all the time or I'll fall apart.*
- *Crying or needing comfort means I am weak.*
- *Trying again just leads to more disappointment.*

CREATIVITY

- **I express myself through art, writing, or imagination.**
- **My ideas matter, even if they are different.**
- **I feel safe to explore, play, and create.**
- **Creativity is seen as a strength.**
- **I am allowed to make messes and try new things.**
- *Creativity is a waste of time—being practical is more important.*
- *I need to stop daydreaming and be realistic.*
- *I believe I am not good at anything creative, so I stop trying.*
- *Making art or expressing feelings is childish or silly.*
- *I feel shame for being different or imaginative.*

BOUNDARIES

- It's okay to say no.
- My body and emotions are respected.
- I speak up if something feels wrong.
- I am allowed to have privacy and space.
- I model healthy limits in relationships.
- *Saying no means I am being selfish or rude.*
- *My feelings and comfort don't matter—I have to go along to get along.*
- *I fear being punished or shamed for setting limits.*
- *I think love means giving everything without question.*
- *Pleasing others is more important than protecting myself.*

ASSERTIVENESS

- It's okay to speak up for myself respectfully.
- My opinions and voice matter.
- I express how I feel, even if it is different from others.
- Being honest and kind can coexist.
- I model healthy communication.
- *Speaking up leads to conflict, so it's safer to stay quiet.*
- *I'll be rejected if I express my true feelings.*
- *Only angry or loud people get their way.*
- *I have to stay small or agreeable to be loved.*
- *Standing up for myself means I am difficult or disrespectful.*

CONFIDENCE

- I try, even if it doesn't turn out as I have planned..
- I believe in myself.
- I am proud of my effort, not just results.
- I feel safe taking risks and asking questions.
- Mistakes are part of growing.
- *If I can't be perfect, I shouldn't even try.*
- *I compare myself to others and feel I don't measure up.*

- *No one believes in me, so I stopped believing in myself.*
- *I feel invisible or dismissed when I speak up.*
- *Confidence is seen as arrogance, so I dim my light.*

INNER PEACE

- **I feel safe and supported by my family, friends, and the Universe, so I feel calm inside.**
- **Even when things are hard, someone is there to help me feel grounded.**
- **It's okay to pause, rest, and listen to myself.**
- **Peace doesn't mean perfection—it means being okay with what is.**
- **Quiet moments are valued, not feared.**
- **The greatest asset I own is the peacefulness within me.**
- *Peace is dangerous—something bad always follows it.*
- *Chaos is normal, so calm feels unfamiliar or unsafe.*
- *I am always on edge, waiting for the next outburst or crisis.*
- *I think anxiety is just part of life.*
- *Stillness makes me feel useless or unproductive.*
- *I strive for more material to feel safer.*

DEPENDABILITY

- **People keep their promises, so I trust and am trustworthy.**
- **I know I can count on someone when I need help.**
- **Being dependable makes me feel valued and connected.**
- **I follow through because it matters to those around me.**
- **I am consistently reliable.**
- *No one ever follows through, so I stopped expecting anything.*
- *If I don't do it myself, it won't get done.*
- *People say one thing and do another—I can't trust anyone.*
- *I am the one everyone depends on, but I have no one to lean on.*
- *Being dependable means being used or taken for granted.*

INTEGRITY

- Telling the truth is valued, even when it is hard.
- I learned that being honest makes me feel proud of who I am
- I do the right thing, even when no one is watching.
- I take responsibility for my actions without shame.
- Keeping my word makes me feel trustworthy and respected.
- *Lying is necessary to avoid punishment.*
- *I say what people want to hear, not what I really feel.*
- *Being honest gets me in trouble, so I stopped being truthful.*
- *Everyone around me is dishonest, so I don't see the point of being honest.*
- *Integrity feels like a burden—no one cares if I do the right thing.*

PATIENCE

- I believe good things can take time.
- Waiting calmly is modeled in my home.
- Others' needs matter too, and sometimes I have to wait.
- Delays don't mean denial—just another step in the process.
- I feel safe even when things don't happen right away.
- Patience allows for others' differences without judgment.
- *If I don't get what I need now, I might never get it.*
- *Patience is for people who got walked on.*
- *No one waits for me, so why should I wait for anyone else?*
- *Delays mean I am not important.*
- *If I don't rush, someone else will take it from me.*
- *I look patient, but I am really just a doormat.*

COURAGE

- I speak up, even when it is hard.
- Bravery means being honest, not being perfect.
- It's okay to be scared and still try.

- I try new things and trust myself.
- Mistakes are part of being brave.
- I have the courage to look within and challenge my limiting beliefs.
- *Speaking up gets me in trouble.*
- *It's safer to stay small and invisible.*
- *If I show how I really feel, I'll be judged or rejected.*
- *Courage means being tough and emotionless.*
- *Vulnerability is dangerous—it makes me weak.*
- *Looking within just opens me up for more pain.*

SELF-DISCIPLINE

- I follow through even when things are hard.
- Being consistent helps me feel proud of myself.
- I manage time and responsibilities.
- Small steps lead to big results.
- I am supported in setting and achieving goals.
- *I am only loved when I perform perfectly.*
- *No one modeled structure, so I had to figure it out alone.*
- *Trying is pointless—I always get it wrong.*
- *I'm lazy and never finish anything.*
- *Discipline means punishment, not support.*

ADAPTABILITY

- Change helps me grow and discover new parts of myself.
- I am flexible and open-minded.
- When things shift, I feel supported in finding a new way.
- I can handle the unexpected.
- Adapting doesn't mean losing myself—it means expanding.
- *I have to constantly adjust to survive.*
- *Nothing ever stays stable, so I stopped trusting anything.*
- *Change means chaos—I learned to fear it.*
- *I have no control over what happens, so I try to control everything.*
- *I am forced to adapt without being asked how I feel.*

PERSEVERANCE

- Effort and patience lead to growth.
- When I fall down, I get back up and try again.
- Persistence builds strength and character.
- Mistakes aren't failures—they are part of learning.
- I keep going, even when it gets hard.
- *No matter how hard I try, it is never enough.*
- *I have to push through everything alone—quitting isn't an option.*
- *Perseverance means exhausting myself to prove my worth.*
- *If I stop, I am weak or a disappointment.*
- *Trying never makes a difference—things stay hard.*

MOTIVATED

- I follow what excites me.
- My passions are seen and supported.
- Doing what I love is worthwhile.
- Effort matters more than perfection.
- I explore what inspires me.
- *I am only motivated by fear of failure or punishment.*
- *I have to please others to feel valuable.*
- *There is no point in trying—it doesn't change anything.*
- *My interests aren't taken seriously.*
- *Motivation doesn't matter—survival does.*

HOPEFULNESS

- I believe things will get better, even when they are hard.
- I look for the good in every situation.
- I hold onto dreams.
- I trust that my future holds promise.
- I see challenges as temporary, not permanent.
- *Hope feels dangerous—it always leads to disappointment.*
- *No one ever showed me things could improve.*
- *Dreaming feels pointless in a world that never changes.*

- *I expect the worst because that's what always happens.*
- *I don't hope because it hurts too much when it doesn't work out.*

SELF-RESPECT

- **My voice and needs matter.**
- **Saying no is a form of self-care.**
- **I am valued for who I am, not just what I do.**
- **I treat myself kindly.**
- **I deserve to be treated with dignity.**
- *I only matter when I please others.*
- *Standing up for myself leads to punishment or rejection.*
- *Self-respect is selfish.*
- *I let others decide my worth.*
- *I have to earn love by ignoring my own needs.*

CONTENTMENT

- **I appreciate what I have.**
- **Joy is found in small, everyday moments.**
- **I don't need more to feel okay—I feel enough.**
- **Being present is more important than being perfect.**
- **Peace comes from within, not from what I own.**
- *There is always something missing, even in good moments.*
- *I believe happiness is for other people, not me.*
- *I always want more—nothing is ever enough.*
- *If I relax, something bad will happen.*
- *Contentment means settling or giving up.*

WHOLENESS

- **I am loved for who I truly am.**
- **I feel accepted, even when I make mistakes.**
- **I don't have to earn love—I already belong.**
- **I bring all parts of myself to the table.**
- **I feel safe being real, not perfect.**

- I seek equal relationships, not one built on codependency.
- I do not make others responsible for my triggers or healing.
- I can leave a relationship with grace and love when it isn't serving my highest and best good.
- *I have to hide parts of myself to be accepted.*
- *If I show my real feelings, I will be rejected.*
- *Only the "good" parts of me are welcome.*
- *I believe I am broken and have to be fixed.*
- *Love is conditional—I have to be who others need me to be.*
- *I seek co-dependent relationships and stay even when I know it's over.*
- *I make others responsible for my wounds and triggers.*
- *I ignore red flags because I don't like to be alone.*

SAFETY

- I feel protected and secure.
- I am emotionally and physically safe.
- It is okay to speak up—I know someone will listen.
- I can relax because I trust the world around me.
- I don't have to be on alert.
- I trust that the world is benevolent and that I am never alone.
- *I always have to watch my back.*
- *No one protects me, so I learned to protect myself.*
- *Crisis is always around the corner—I never feel safe.*
- *I can't trust others to have my best interest in mind.*
- *Being vulnerable is dangerous.*
- *I am always in fight/flight/fawn mode.*

Exercise 4

Writing Your Story, Part 1

✳

WHEN THESE BELIEFS began, more often than not, you were a young child without the emotional and psychological resources to challenge these beliefs. Worse, these beliefs became a part of how you viewed yourself and the world, often at a deep subconscious level, so you may not even be aware that your wounded self is running the show.

In this exercise, I would like you to take the messages you believed and write your life story. Please try to be as brutally honest as possible, even if some of the limiting beliefs or lessons you've learned might not be positive about yourself and difficult to admit.

It is important to recognize that these messages began when you were a young, innocent, trusting child, especially if the harmful messages were coming from the very people who were supposed to protect you.

There is no judgment in healing work, and, from a spiritual perspective, there is no judgment at all. Our Higher Power sees everything as a lesson to be learned. From a Soul perspective, with each authentic step towards lifting the illusions and limiting beliefs you have been living behind, you can become closer to your best, truest self and return your inner child to its original state of joyful, unconditional love and innocence.

I will provide an example as a guideline from my past experience.

A Story from My Childhood Programming

From the age of six to seven, I believed I had no one I could depend on, so I had to rely on myself. *Trust no one, even myself; check and double-check.* This was my motto. If I wanted to keep Mother alive and my brothers safe, I needed to be the perfect child and helper because Mother had such a hard life, and I was a burden.

There was no room in my family for authentic emotions. I needed to bury who I was, to become who I needed to be, to survive in my family. I had no boundaries and felt that I was there to serve others' needs over my own. Mother lived in a state of victimhood my entire life, so I needed to be self-sufficient, resilient, assertive, courageous, and optimistic, burying any negative emotion or fear I felt.

I learned that a chaotic environment and toxic relationships were my "normal," so I sought these types of relationships. I believed that asking for my needs to be met was selfish, so I didn't practice self-care. My childhood was so chaotic that I didn't learn how to make choices that were in my highest and best interest. Instead, I learned that I must take what life offers and make the best of it; I became a pro at reactive life management.

I never felt physically threatened; however, I shut down my emotions so I could feel safe from the emotional toll of my family environment, existing in a high-anxiety environment at all times. From a young age, creativity was an innate part of my personality. However, this, too, became a forgotten quality, as the aliveness of my creativity was too much for my family to handle. So, I learned to "dampen" my Light to make everyone else more comfortable.

I felt blessed with an incredible amount of gratitude, striving to feel blessed for what I have and not live by my family's edict of "what I don't have." My parents were not honest during my childhood, and as a method to survive, I always denied this about them; I trust too easily.

My curiosity needs were strong, and I became an avid reader at a young age, which helped me stay sane in insane circumstances. I had to learn to take care of myself at a very young age. I am self-confident, which propelled me through college and my adult life.

Inner peace was never a goal. I was the proverbial hamster on a wheel, trying to reach the next goal and not stopping to feel what was brewing beneath the surface. There was never a "resting" place after I met a goal. It was moving from one goal to the next, so I wouldn't have to feel.

Patience was not a tremendous asset for most of my life; I was very controlling, Type A, and I worked to get things done quickly, not appreciating that many walked differently. I kept my impatience to myself except when I was with my husband.

I was always willing to help and give. Sports became an outlet for my stress, and running was a way for me to find calm and validation outside myself. Running taught me self-discipline and inner fortitude.

I always felt it necessary to save as much as possible because underneath it all, I always felt unsafe, so I was always planning for tomorrow. I did not understand that the only safety was from within. Forgiveness was a simple thing for me since I had forgiven my family of origin a million times over. I forgave quickly to be revered as a "good girl." I forgave others even when I should have walked away to protect myself.

Conflict management in business was a strong suit; however, I wasn't great at this on a personal level because I never learned the "how" to navigate conflict in intimate relationships. Instead, I just agreed or severed ties out of hurt, ending relationships rather than deal with the discomfort of conflict. I am very adaptable by nature, maybe even more so since my life was in constant chaos and motion. I can handle any change that comes my way. I have total self-control under all situations because I have become adept at burying my emotions and staying emotionally detached. To me, contentment is feeling safe, juggling all the balls in the air, and reaching each goal to move on to the next.

Now, it's your turn to write your story. As with the previous exercises, it is important that you find a quiet place to tackle this with an open mind and honesty. If you find it hard to go back, take a few deep breaths and focus your attention on your heart space/heart chakra, and ask your Higher Power, spirit guides, and guardian angels for guidance in writing your childhood story; they are all there to help you grow and heal and will provide the support you need.

Once you feel centered and balanced and have a clear head, write your story using the knowledge you gained from the previous exercises. For many of you, you might have shed some of your limiting beliefs. This is fine. You should include them as well, as I have done. It is important to recognize your growth even if you are no longer in that space.

_____

_____

_____

_____

_____

_____

_____

_____

_____

_____

_____

_____

_____

_____

Exercise 5

Limiting Beliefs

✻

YOU HAVE A blueprint of how you learned to navigate life based on the false beliefs you adopted. Now, it's time to delve into the impact these limiting beliefs have had on your adult life. In this exercise, you are not trying to understand. You are simply trying to focus on what your adult life has been like, and you have no judgment or thought as to "the why" you should go into this exercise.

I have included an example of how I parented because of the above:

Parenting Style Example

I tried to parent the opposite of my parents and took over too many of my kids' emotional challenges, rather than let them fall. I wanted everything to be "perfect" for my kids, for them to be all they could be. Sometimes this was good; sometimes it was bad.

In all aspects of my kids' lives, I become emotionally invested. I shielded them from anything negative that I could. My kids learned the value of being frugal. I taught my kids the necessity of hard work and that no one owes them anything. My over-involvement enabled them, which negatively impacted them as they entered college and were on their own, especially my older son.

I allowed my kids to believe that we measure success externally. I taught my kids that service and giving back are essential parts of life. I did not allow any sense of entitlement in my home. I gave them a model for marriage that was not functional, so my kids believed that women did everything and that men only did what they liked. I showed my kids that giving up is not acceptable.

I loved them fully and tried to encourage self-expression. We spoke about emotions in our home, but not extensively. I never allowed my kids to see me be vulnerable. We allowed differences of opinion. Religion was part of my kids' lives, though their own opinions were supported. I encouraged friendships and supported their friendships in every way possible. I encouraged my kids to stretch themselves and to seize every opportunity.

I lived in high stress 24/7, so this is what my boys felt. I never shared my past with my kids, not wanting to ruin their innocence. I kept my late husband's alcohol addiction hidden from my kids. We created many wonderful childhood memories despite these challenges.

I taught my boys that women have no limitations. I taught my boys that a woman can do the work of a man. I taught my boys the value of home maintenance and the importance of not being

> afraid to do things yourself. I taught my boys the value of planning for the future, saving for the future, delaying gratification when purchasing anything other than a necessity, and not relying on credit.
>
> I taught my boys that each member of the family must do their part. I taught my boys that their relationship with each other was paramount. I "made" my boys watch each other's activities, when appropriate, so they could develop a shared history even though they were almost eight years apart.
>
> I instructed my boys to respect their relatives, even when they might not receive the same respect in return. I taught my boys that they should share their friends' successes. I taught my boys to be available for good and bad in their friends' lives. I taught my boys gratitude.

As with the previous exercises, it is important that you find a quiet place to tackle this with an open mind and honesty. If you are finding it hard to go back, take a few deep breaths and focus your attention on your heart space/heart chakra, and ask your Higher Power, spirit guides, and guardian angels for guidance in writing your childhood story; they are all there to help you grow and heal and will provide the support you need.

Once you feel centered and balanced and have a clear head, write your story using the knowledge you gained from the previous exercises. For many of you, you might have shed some of your limiting beliefs. This is fine. You should include them as well, as I have done. It is important to recognize your growth even if you are no longer in that space.

Please describe the following in as much emotional detail as possible.

College or First Work Experience

Later College or Work Experience

First Intimate Relationship

First Heartbreak

Second/Third/Fourth Serious Relationship(s)

Long-Term Committed Relationship/Marriage

Decision to Have Children or Not

Parenting Style

Friendships

Faith/Religion

Work or Career Changes

Conflict Management Style in Relationships

Relationship With Parent(s)

Relationship With Sibling(s)/Extended Family

Self-Care/Health/Wellness

Relationship to Money and Finances

Exercise 6

Patterns

✺

THIS EXERCISE INVOLVES trying to understand the patterns that your childhood limiting beliefs and false programming have created. In this exercise, you will write the story honestly and authentically. There should be no judgment toward yourself. The intent is to acknowledge the patterns so we can begin creating a life story based on truth and not the false messages they taught you.

My Childhood Limiting Beliefs and False Programming

In my life, I felt a deeply buried shame and attracted men who needed to feel adored and mothered, me giving a lot and them giving a little. I accepted this because my "version" of love was exactly this model. I accepted poor treatment and immature behavior, forgiving easily because I learned this as a child. I asked for no needs to be met because by now, I believed I had no needs; childhood largely convinced me of this.

My primary goal in choosing partners was to find peace from the chaos of my childhood, and each romantic relationship morphed into a parent-child arrangement, in which I was quite familiar. I didn't believe I was worthy of anything more.

By the end of each, which was always done by me after I had grown enough to want more, I would leave freely, though I never really understood the why, so future relationships repeated themselves. I never had a romantic partner who had my back, supported me, challenged me, was emotionally present, listened, put my needs first or equal, or carried their weight, whether physically or emotionally; all this I accepted as normal.

I chose my college largely because of the location—it was close to my boyfriend's college, and I couldn't imagine being away from him. The school was not my best choice as I had larger running scholarship offers from better colleges. My parents did not provide any support toward my college goals, so I decided from an emotionally wounded place.

I felt accepted in high school and college, but had no "true" friends because I never allowed myself to be vulnerable—I did not know that was the case. Most friendships were me supporting the other; again, this felt comfortable.

My first career choice was in a field I knew nothing about; however, I was adept at communicating with adults and landed the position before I returned home from the interview. This began a long career in finance that was financially rewarding but had no impact on me on a Soul level.

Until my husband's death, I never really admitted how much I actually disliked the field. Clients, peers, and management highly regarded me and considered me very successful, as my veneer was that of a Type A, hard-charging, and goal-oriented individual. I made a lot of money, but I was extremely frugal; money meant safety, and I never saw it as a means to personal material fulfillment. This allowed me to save a lot, beginning very early.

When I met my husband, bells and whistles didn't go off, but we were in step immediately; it was as if we had been together forever and were just picking up where we left off. Our childhood wounds were complementary, as deeply rooted and damaging, though unconscious.

Chuck believed he came from an idyllic childhood, so I saw him as better than me for quite some time. Our long-term goals of having children and raising them in a traditional environment were a huge connection, and before long, we were well on our way.

I had no illusions about getting my needs met in the marriage, still operating the parent/child paradigm of love. Chuck was happy to play the role of child. I was the ultimate codependent and felt the relationship would meet my needs to continue supporting my childhood family financially; Chuck never impeded this need.

I had plenty of friends, though in retrospect I had none, because I could only support a one-sided relationship. My husband "forbade" me from talking about how his alcoholism affected our marriage and family, convincing me it would damage our financial services business. With ease, I kept my husband's secret, having kept my family's secrets my entire life.

We had limited couples' friends, and as our marriage progressed, we became a more closed unit. Enmeshed is a term I would use today, though I didn't see it then. As the kids came, the focus shifted to raising children. I took my role as a parent seriously and was 100 percent focused on doing the very opposite of my parents. I loved both boys to the fullest extent and placed a lot of attention on mitigating any type of emotional pain that they might feel, enabling both my husband and my kids, more so my oldest son.

By the time my youngest was two, Mother had just passed, and I had had enough with Chuck's drinking since it was affecting our kids. I assumed if he stopped drinking, he would become a higher-functioning family member. I did not fully understand that we were both complicit in our drama: I was over-responsible; Chuck was under-responsible. We were in perfect balance.

After he stopped drinking, things actually began a slow decline until his death. Chuck's crutch was gone, so I became his primary crutch, along with his reliance on trading our money in the stock market for the "high" of a windfall; this, too, I didn't understand until after his death. We each had our own method of escape: my achievements, his in the stock market. We were both blind to ourselves and each other and the false programming that ran the show.

From the outside looking in, we had it all. It wasn't until the last several years before Chuck's death that I started growing and needing more emotional depth when things really declined. Still, I didn't understand what was happening. Periodically, I felt a deep sense of complete unhappiness on a Soul level. I had no experience understanding this as a cry from within, so I just ignored and buried it when it came up.

Friendships were becoming more authentic, but if a conflict arose, with limited conflict resolution skills, I typically just severed the relationship or distanced myself instead of trying to work it out maturely. Family shame, both past and current, still ruled my life and inner messages.

Mostly, I felt disconnected from myself and others, as I was unaware, since this was all I knew. I gave to my community and

> the global world regularly from a place of survivor's guilt for having so much compared to my family and others; many took advantage of this worldview.
>
> I can't say I was overtly unhappy because my life was infinitely better than my childhood and, by society's standards, perfect. I believed society knew better than I.

Start writing your story in the space provided, remembering to stay honest and authentic without judgment.

Life Story from False Programming

Rewriting the Stories that Shape Our Lives

Exercise 7

Defense Mechanisms

✸

WHEN WE GROW up in a dysfunctional environment, we are so vulnerable to painful and conflicting emotions. As a method to survive and not feel too overwhelmed, we often resort to defense mechanisms: "psychological strategies that are unconsciously used to protect a person from anxiety arising from unacceptable thoughts or feelings."[5]

When reacting from a place of unconsciousness, you cut off a large part of your authentic self, inhibiting your emotional growth. Negative defenses prevent you from knowing and expressing what you are actually feeling; as a result, you become hidden from yourself and everyone else. Often feeling constricted, it's easy to lose the ability to create the life your Soul desires.

Some defense mechanisms can be positive, such as engaging in a distraction, as long as it isn't obsessive. Others block your truth, such as compartmentalizing, separating experiences into different parts of your memory. This serves to avoid uncomfortable emotions. An example of a positive defense would be to watch a comedy or read a book to destress by taking your mind off an emotionally stressful situation. This allows you to cope effectively with our current reality by being mindful and emotionally present.

Defenses can arise at any point in your life. However, the defenses from childhood are the most insidious and potentially damaging to fulfilling relationships and to being able to live as your best self. Being aware of how you defend against your emotions, conflicts, and confrontations allows you to move past them, allowing you to move closer to wholeness.

From the list of various defense mechanisms below, discover which ones you used during childhood and continue to use regularly to help you support your false programming. Please be as brutally honest as possible and understand there is no judgment on the path to healing; uncovering the truth helps us change our story permanently.

Check all that apply.

Common Defense Mechanisms

- Spacing out
- Not listening
- Criticizing
- Perfectionism
- Judging self/others
- Negative thinking
- Procrastination
- Excessive working
- Sarcasm
- Humor
- Displacement
- Obsessions
- Changing the subject
- Laughing
- Stockholm syndrome
- Lying
- Manipulation
- Omnipotence
- Addiction (drugs, alcohol, gambling, exercising, food, relationships, shopping, hoarding, etc.)
- Numbing of emotions
- Secretiveness
- Helplessness
- Evasiveness
- Deflection
- Denial
- Projection
- Repression
- Sublimation
- Racism
- Prejudice
- Preoccupation
- Rationalization
- Splitting
- Devaluation
- Idealization
- Silent treatment
- Aggression
- Controlling behavior

Exercise 8

Labeling Defense Mechanisms

✺

NOW THAT YOU have identified the defense mechanisms you have used to manage the chaos of your childhood and the defenses that perhaps have carried over into adulthood, it's time to label them as positive or negative. A positive defense would be to break the tension with a joke, and a negative one would be to joke constantly to avoid any "serious" interaction.

You can't change what you don't know, and conversely, you can't unsee what you see. Once you discover how you move through life, it becomes much easier to respond with more beneficial reactions and authentic interactions.

Positive Defenses

Negative Defenses

Exercise 9

Reflect on Relationships

✸

CERTAIN EVENTS FROM dysfunctional childhoods cause the most pain, and if they aren't dealt with on a conscious level, they can trigger the same emotions in all future relationships. Unconsciously, we take our triggers out on the people we love the most and are closest to, often unjustifiably.

One of my biggest childhood triggers is abandonment, so for much of my life, I hung onto relationships that were not in my highest good and best interest. And if the relationship ended, even if I knew it was for the better, it would often trigger a deep emotional response that did not correlate with the current relationship or situation.

Until I recognized the wound as being open from childhood and not a current emotional reaction, I hung onto toxic relationships, long-expired friendships, and even career positions that weren't in my best interest. Being able to identify the emotion as current or a residual from our wounded child is a significant step towards healing those wounds and finding the wholeness that is our birthright.

In this exercise, I would like you to find a calm space and reflect on your relationship situations (romantic, children, friends, work) and recall some reactions you have had to circumstances. The easiest way to narrow down potential triggers is to reflect on the defenses you have used and try to determine the emotion you were trying to avoid.

Was the emotion a current feeling, or did it bring you back to an emotion you experienced in childhood? If it is current, it is not a trigger; if it elicits an emotional reaction from childhood, write it down without judgment.

For many, you will have an awareness of these triggers; for others, these triggers might come as a total shock that your past, wounded child is still running the show. Never should you feel ashamed or any other negative emotion. If you feel anything, I hope you feel relief because this brings you closer to grieving what wounded your inner child and finally healing those wounds that have been open far too long.

Do this exercise as extensively as you can, reflecting on all meaningful relationships, including romantic, children, friendships, and work.

Defenses Commonly Used In Past/Current Relationships

_____
_____
_____
_____
_____
_____
_____

Were/are the reaction(s) proportionate with the current situation?

_____
_____
_____
_____
_____
_____
_____
_____

Did the exchange trigger a reaction you can recall from childhood?

_____
_____
_____
_____
_____
_____
_____
_____

Is there a pattern or common theme to your triggers?

_____
_____
_____
_____
_____
_____
_____
_____

Exercise 10

Write Your Story, Part 2

✺

ONCE YOU HAVE identified your triggers, it's now time to write your story from the adult perspective, who can objectively see the wounded child. Most times, the Universe provides opportunities to help us heal, and I am certain the right people came into my life at exactly the right time to help me feel the childhood wounds acutely so I could take the steps to heal them.

Nobody crosses our path randomly, nor are relationships simply lucky or unlucky. Every interaction has a lesson to learn and a pattern to help us break until our wounds heal. Patterns are ways of attracting the same person/relationship/career over and over until we finally see the pattern and learn the lesson.

Unearthed emotional triggers from childhood provide the fastest way towards healing if we pay attention. If we don't, the same people or circumstances will continue crossing our paths until we stop, take notice, grieve, and heal.

Childhood Triggers Example

Besides my abandonment issues, I have needed to be the best at everything. If anyone ever criticized me, I would feel a tremendous sense of shame, a shame that was never commiserate with the intention of the criticism. The criticism was triggering my childhood shame and my overall sense of feeling worthless and unlovable. Not winning or succeeding was never an option for the same reasons.

Once I realized my weak boundaries with others, particularly in intimate relationships, I became overly reactive even when the offense was relatively mild. The trigger was how people treated me in childhood and how people never respected my boundaries; my inner child was angry and reacted accordingly. Even today, as healed as I am, I catch myself feeling deeply hurt when someone I love and who I believe loves me, does not "see me" in my truth. I am aware of this, so I can temper it with my adult self. However, I still feel the residual pain of never being "seen" in childhood. As time goes on, this softens, and it has become a great resource to know when someone is safe to trust with my heart.

Speaking of trust, this is another trigger I have had to overcome. Because my entire childhood was based on a continuous series of lies and broken promises, I had to convince myself, because of my sensitivity, that things weren't as bad as they seemed and that "this time they are telling the truth." Nobody mirrored or affirmed my feelings, so I ignored my inner guidance and intuition, often choosing to trust untrustworthy people.

Historically, I was too trusting and was taken advantage of or manipulated. Even if the infraction was small, there would be a huge emotional response being brought into my awareness, triggered by the acute dishonesty I suffered as a young girl.

Discernment has also been a central theme in my life, serving as another trigger. Historically, I have had a tendency to overlook red flags in most situations, not believing that when people told or showed me who they were, I needed to believe them. I used to choose to ignore the rough edges (red flags) and focus on the innate potential I saw at the Soul level. Most times, despite the hurt I experienced, I was triggered to keep trying repeatedly with a person who had no willingness or desire to grow. In reality, not everyone cares to change.

The frustration I have felt, even in the face of the obvious, was a clear trigger; I kept giving my parents chance after chance to do better, to no avail, causing me pain today from something that was still lingering from childhood.

Your Childhood Trigger Story

Exercise 11

Affirmations

✺

NOW THAT YOU have identified your triggers, you have also identified your wounds. This is the most exciting part of your journey because this is the place where healing can occur. Before proceeding, though, it is important for me to reiterate a few basic facts to help you reach a place where you actually believe in healing.

Throughout my five-decade journey, the vast majority of my life, if not all of it, I have believed in a Higher Power. I knew there was someone or something greater than me, even if I didn't really grasp the full meaning. After Chuck died, I went through "the dark night of the soul," which was my prelude to my spiritual awakening. During the first several years, I spent an intense amount of time in therapy, reading books, receiving afterlife messages, and soul searching, essentially questioning everything I thought I knew to be true.

I had the luxury of two very important relationships after Chuck's death, both of which caused a lot of pain but uncovered my deeply buried childhood wounds. Both men I loved and in their own ways broke my heart wide open. In healing, I found peace as I connected with my Higher Self and the Divine, which I believe resides within all of us.

Along the way, I learned we are all gifted with wholeness on a Soul level, and we all have exactly what we need to heal our wounds. We are called to do this as part of our journey on this wonderful planet.

Feeling connected to our Higher Self and whatever we call our Divine (God, Source, the Divine, Buddha, Krishna, the Universe, Allah, etc.) is a catalyst for full healing. The name is irrelevant; what is relevant is finding that inner peace that comes from a place of love rather than fear.

Love is why we are here, and love is truly all that matters. When you live from a state of childhood triggers and wounds, you are essentially living in fear, and fear is the exact opposite of love and what your Soul and Higher Self seek—you can see how much havoc this would cause! When you realize that everyone has been approaching this from a flawed perspective, seeking wholeness from a place of fear, external desires, wishes, and hopes, you can then turn your attention inward toward your own inner world, which is the only way to heal.

There is no such thing as finding wholeness; we are already whole the minute we are born—we have never not been whole. Childhood, young adult experiences, societal expectations, inborn temperament, and our reaction to our environments all add layers of "wet blankets" onto our light, never completely snuffing it out, but hiding it in such a way that we no longer experience that light.

At some point, we believe the light is outside ourselves, that it is for the select few, and we must find it. As we heal, we remove the "wet blankets" layer by layer, revealing what has always been there: a place of peace, joy, contentment, connection to ourselves and our Source, and an undeniable, unconditional love for ourselves and others.

Would our Source give this only to some and not to the others? Is this for the select few? Absolutely not! This is for all of us, and why we are here. It is critical you believe in this truth. This is not my truth. It is all of our truth. It is the truth of being a spiritual being, having a human experience.

For many of us, the idea that we are whole and worthy of deep love and connection to all might seem both impossible and foreign. So, we need to start changing that thought system, which is a leftover from childhood programming. We lie to ourselves that we are broken, implying that we need to be put back together. This is completely false.

Daily Affirmations

Affirmations and positive words have significance in changing our beliefs and even healing molecules on a cellular level, so the more positive thoughts we can bring into our awareness, the better. Below is a list of sample affirmations. Feel free to use any of these or come up with some of your own.

> No matter my size, shape, or age, I am beautiful.
> I am worthy of feeling deep, unconditional self-love.
> I deserve to be treated with respect.
> My boundaries keep me safe and are valid.
> My intuition is a connection to my Higher Power, and I will find strength in listening.
> All the answers I need are inside me; I choose to listen to my inner wisdom and voice.
> I will ask for what I need from my higher power, spirit guides, and guardian angels.
> I know I am never alone.
> I see the beauty in nature and feel my connection to all that is.
> My inner light shines brightly even when I don't see or feel it.
> It is my God given right to feel whole and loved.
> I choose to live in Love and not fear.
> I forgive myself for anything I have done out of fear vs. love.
> I forgive others for everything they have done out of fear vs. love.
> I feel gratitude for all that I have.
> I will offer kindness to all who cross my path.
> I do not judge myself.
> I do not judge others.
> I am enough simply by being.
> I do not believe the false messages I have been told.
> I know that the people who hurt me did the best they could.

> The only thing my Source asks of me is to be my truest, most authentic self.
> I am emotionally strong and willing to be vulnerable.
> I accept everyone as they are.
> I will live this day with childlike wonder and curiosity.
> I will choose inner peace over external wealth.
> I will live today with a sense of deep hope.
> I will pray for others.
> I will pray for myself, knowing self-care equates self-love.
> I am a child of my Divine, and I am good.
> I am grateful for all that I have.

By now, I hope you have already begun incorporating these affirmations into your life. The goal of these daily affirmations is to change your subconscious, so eventually you actually start believing in their truth. This is not an overnight process, but rather a slow unwinding of your false beliefs, essentially reprogramming your self-perception.

When you say these words to yourself, whether in your head or out loud, I want you to feel them deeply in your heart space, rather than your head space. Ponder how each feels to you, experience the emotions each affirmation elicits, challenge yourself to experience the rawness of your programming, and let the words help you heal your wounds.

If you go deep enough, you might experience emotions that surprise you. You may feel sadness when confronted with your true feelings about yourself and others. Or you might feel anger knowing how misled you were and conditioned to believe things about yourself that were not true.

Please don't rush this or shy away from this. Stay with it and feel what you need to feel. Part of the false programming stems from not healing the inner child wounds; part of healing those wounds involves experiencing the pain around them and acknowledging how your innocent inner child was affected.

When necessary, take a break, but always know your adult is now in charge and has the emotional skills and connection to your Higher Power to navigate any emotion that comes your way. Our Soul truly has all that it needs to heal.

If you're feeling at all anxious or deeply emotional during this process, take a moment to dialog with your inner child and let him or her know they are safe, no one can harm them anymore, that you have their back, that you love them unconditionally, that you will never leave them or let them down. Say this with conviction as many times as necessary until you feel a sense of peace wash over you. Then continue.

This exercise has no ending because these affirmations become a part of your ongoing daily life as you move toward fully healing. While you might not overtly practice this list as time goes on, as you heal, you will live each of these affirmations daily. You will find a renewed sense of energy, and energy that emanates from your inner Soul and shines brightly to all who come in contact with you.

When you have reached a place where you believe each of these affirmations on a deep soul level, you are ready to rewrite your story and acknowledge proudly that your programming has changed.

My Daily Affirmations

Exercise 12

Anthem

✸

NOW, YOU ARE ready to rewrite your story—a story based on Truth, coming from your Higher Self and Unconditional Self-Love. Let this flow freely from your heart. Let your words become your Anthem for a new way of experiencing life. I wrote my new Anthem first as a guideline. Have fun with this. See this as a liberation from all the programming that has held you back. Allow your new Anthem to become the song of your Higher Self.

Remember: We are all whole and always have been.

My New Anthem

I am beautiful both inside and out. I live my life as authentically as possible, knowing that each day I become more myself, as my Source has made me. I am grateful for my connection to my inner light and the unconditional love I feel towards myself and the rest of the world.

I take joy in the simple things each day and feel a sense of peace that I never thought possible. I can enter meaningful, deeply enriching, intimate relationships of all kinds, where everyone respects each other's boundaries, love is based on equality, and vulnerability is the norm.

I do not live in the past or the future. Today is all that there is, so I fear nothing. I have forgiven myself for everything I have or haven't done, and I forgive everyone else as well. I recognize we are all doing the very best we can at any given moment, and I respect where each of us is on our respective journeys.

When I feel off balance, I go inside and seek support from my intuition and wisdom, asking for guidance from my Higher Power, Spirit Guides, and Guardian Angels. I pray for others and myself, as well, knowing that one can't receive if one doesn't ask. I have patience for others along the way, and I try to meet them where they are, sometimes being the teacher, and other times, the student. I feel deep gratitude for the people who have entered my life and have been instrumental in my growth, even when it has been painful.

No emotion is wrong, and I judge none. I feel each and every thing, and then I release it. I no longer feel the need to form attachments to material things and the people I love. I love from a place of want, not need.

I am emotionally resilient and deeply sensitive at the same time; I don't need walls to keep me feeling safe. My heart chakra has opened, and I am blessed. I can feel so much more deeply and experience the richness of life in such a meaningful, profound way. I see the beauty in nature and strive to commune with nature daily. I feel a deep connection to my Higher Power and know without a doubt that heaven is within us all.

I give from a place of abundance, guided by my heart. I feel the world in all its splendor and approach every day with the curiosity of a child and the discernment of an adult. I have learned that everything I want and desire is already within me. Inner Peace, Joy, and Unconditional Love are our true homeostasis.

I am learning the lessons I came here to learn, recognizing that learning is lifelong, and I will keep growing as I deepen my connection to all. I will be a beacon of Hope and Light to others on their journey.

Your New Anthem

Conclusion: A Return to Wholeness

It's not how you started your life; it's how you decide to live it. By showing up for yourself and doing this work, you've taken a brave and beautiful step toward reclaiming your truth. The stories that once shaped your sense of self no longer have to define you. You have learned how to meet your inner world with compassion, curiosity, and courage. You've begun to uncover the layers—those wet blankets of limiting beliefs—and beneath them, you've remembered what was always there: your wholeness.

This workbook wasn't about "fixing" you; you were never broken. It was about creating space to see yourself clearly, through the eyes of love rather than fear, through truth rather than programming. Each exercise, each affirmation, each pause you took to feel and heal has been a homecoming.

You now have tools to navigate your inner landscape, to gently question the inherited narratives, and to choose again, from a place of empowerment. The subconscious mind is powerful, yes—but so is your intention. Repetition, awareness, and presence are the keys to rewriting what's been written by others.

Your story is no longer bound by the past. It is being rewritten in real time—by you.

So, keep affirming your truth. Keep listening inward. Keep walking in the direction of peace, joy, and inner freedom. Heaven is not a destination; it's a remembrance. It lives within you now.

This is your new story: *I am whole. I am worthy. I am free.*

Endnotes

1. Timothy D. Wilson, *Strangers to Ourselves: Discovering the Adaptive Unconscious* (Cambridge, MA: Harvard University Press, 2022).
2. Helen Schucman and William Thetford, *Course in Miracles* (Omaha, NE: Course in Miracles Society, 2009).
3. A. H. Maslow, "A Theory of Human Motivation.," *Psychological Review* 50, no. 4 (July 1943): 370–96, https://doi.org/10.1037/h0054346.
4. Alan D. Wolfelt, "Mustering the Courage to Mourn," Center for Loss & Life Transition, December 21, 2023, https://www.centerforloss.com/2023/12/mustering-courage-mourn/.
5. Saul McLeod, "Defense Mechanisms in Psychology Explained," Simply Psychology, January 25, 2024, https://www.simplypsychology.org/defense-mechanisms.html.

Acknowledgments

I am deeply grateful to the many wonderful individuals whose love, wisdom, and support have guided me throughout my spiritual journey and the writing of this book.

I would like to express my deepest gratitude to Igniting Souls for providing the most meaningful platform to bring my book to life. Your expertise throughout the publishing journey has been invaluable. Thank you for believing in my vision and helping make it a reality.

To my husband, Chuck, with sincere gratitude and love for giving me the very best curriculum for learning in the school of life. Our life together has afforded me the opportunity for the greatest growth and has provided my most valuable lessons, for which I thank you.

A special thank you to Rosalie Strawcutter, a gifted clairvoyant medium, whose insights have helped me understand my life in profound and meaningful ways. You mean the world to me, and I am proud to call you friend. To my spiritual sister, Mary Greene, your unwavering presence and love have been an anchor through it all. Joe Cimoch, your wisdom in leading ACIM has illuminated my path and provided clarity at every turn.

I want to express my deepest gratitude to my friend, Jeff DeRoberts. Through all the ups and downs of life, Jeff has been by my side, offering support, laughter, and friendship when I needed it most. Our bond is unshakeable, and it's impossible to imagine this journey without him.

I would like to thank Bob Peters for graciously allowing us to meet each week at Phoenix Books Clintonville, a space that nurtures growth and community. Nancy Kirchofer, your beautiful facilitation of Dr. Hawkins' teachings has helped me see the world with new eyes.

To my dear book group friends—Madonna, David, Marilyn, Bob, Rahkee, Chetan, Rich, Trish, Andrew, Joseph, Maggie, Katherine, Rev. Clarence, Rebecca, Jim, and Doug—thank you for being such a loving and supportive witness to my spiritual journey and for helping me along this path.

I am incredibly grateful to Gail Lichtenfels for opening Epic Books each Thursday night for our Yellow Springs ACIM group, providing a space for learning and connection.

To my many dear friends, especially Krista, Samantha, Brenda, Beth, Scott, Steve, Deb, Rita, Bill, and Anne, your love and friendship have been a constant source of strength and encouragement.

Thank you to Rebecca Manns, Angel Reader, for your spiritual guidance and unwavering support. Mystic Laura Scott, your energy healings and support in helping me discover my life plan have been transformative and truly invaluable. I would like to extend my heartfelt thanks to Psychic Medium Bee Herz for your insightful guidance. Your wisdom has been instrumental in navigating a path toward a more beneficial and fulfilling future.

I would like to express my deepest gratitude to the First Community Church Youth Program and Camp Akita for the unwavering support you have provided to my children and for the profound impact you've had on our lives. Your guidance, care, and unconditional love have not only shaped their growth but have also supported me in ways that words can hardly express.

To my brothers, David, Kenny, and Bruce, and their spouses, Paul (David) and Debi (Bruce), your light in my life has been a constant source of joy and grounding. To Patty, Jeff, Steven, Marcia, Amelia, Kayla, and Colton, thank you for understanding the true value of family and for always being there with love and support.

A heartfelt thank you to Tim, Sharon, Sarah (Alex), Rachel (Alex), Tom, Jane, Chris, and Judy for your continued efforts to maintain a strong relationship with my boys, which has been a great support to me.

To each of you, I offer my heartfelt gratitude. Your presence has helped shape my journey, and I could not have done this without you.

With love and appreciation,
Tricia

About the Author

Tricia Baxley is a passionate advocate for personal growth and healing with over 25 years of experience in the financial services industry and transformational life coaching. A devoted mother of two amazing boys, Tricia holds degrees in finance and psychology, which have shaped her unique approach to understanding human behavior. In her book, she shares her personal journey from trauma to triumph, exploring the stories we tell ourselves and uncovering the limiting beliefs that hold us back.

Tricia is a Certified MBTI Practitioner and a Certified Life Coach, empowering others to overcome obstacles and embrace their full potential. She is a proud member of the International Coaching Alliance, dedicating her life to helping others heal and achieve lasting transformation. Tricia's commitment to serving others is deeply rooted in her belief in the power of personal development and the impact of self-awareness on all aspects of life. Through her work, she continues to inspire those around her to break free from their limitations and create a life of purpose and fulfillment. In addition to her professional pursuits, Tricia is passionate about mission work, intentional travel, and running, which fuels her drive to connect with others and explore the world with purpose.

BRING TRICIA TO YOUR NEXT EVENT

Tricia Baxley speaks from a place of lived experience, emotional depth, and spiritual insight. Her talks invite listeners to gently uncover their unconscious beliefs, embrace their authentic selves, and remember their innate wholeness.

To book Tricia to speak, visit:

Apath4Healing.com

DISCOVER PERSONALIZED COACHING SESSIONS

Work one-on-one with Tricia in a sacred, compassionate space where deep inner patterns can rise to the surface and be gently rewritten. This is not about fixing — it's about remembering who you were before the world told you otherwise.

Apath4Healing.com

GROUP WORKSHOPS/ RETREATS

Experience heart-centered, collaborative workshops designed to awaken truth, foster healing, and invite soul-level transformation through shared stories, guided inquiry, and sacred connection.

Apath4Healing.com

DO YOU FEEL DISCONNECTED FROM YOURSELF?

Through her personal journey of healing and awakening, Tricia gently guides you to release the limiting stories you've carried — and return to the truth of who you are: whole, worthy, and powerful beyond the narratives you've outgrown.

THIS BOOK IS PROTECTED INTELLECTUAL PROPERTY

The author of this book values Intellectual Property. The book you just read is protected by Instant IP[IP], a proprietary process, which integrates blockchain technology giving Intellectual Property "Global Protection." By creating a "Time-Stamped" smart contract that can never be tampered with or changed, we establish "First Use" that tracks back to the author.

Instant IP[IP] functions much like a Pre-Patent since it provides an immutable "First Use" of the Intellectual Property. This is achieved through our proprietary process of leveraging blockchain technology and smart contracts. As a result, proving "First Use" is simple through a global and verifiable smart contract. By protecting intellectual property with blockchain technology and smart contracts, we establish a "First to File" event.

Protected by Instant IP[IP]

LEARN MORE AT INSTANTIP.TODAY